Henry S.

CLUB
ICARUS

CLUB
ICARUS

Poems by Matt W. Miller

2012 WINNER, VASSAR MILLER PRIZE IN POETRY

[signature]
1/24/2014
Deerfield

UNT PRESS

University of North Texas Press, Denton, Texas

.ler

.1.
Jnited States of America.

6 5 4 3 2

Permissions:
University of North Texas Press
1155 Union Circle #311336
Denton, TX 76203-5017

The paper used in this book meets the minimum requirements of the American National
Standard for Permanence of Paper for Printed Library Materials, z39.48.1984. Bind-
ing materials have been chosen for durability.

Library of Congress Cataloging-in-Publication Data

Miller, Matt W., 1973–
  Club Icarus : poems / by Matt W. Miller.—1st ed.
    p. cm.—(Vassar Miller Prize in Poetry series ; no. 20)
  2012 Winner, Vassar Miller Prize in Poetry.
  ISBN 978-1-57441-504-9 (pbk. : alk. paper)—ISBN 978-1-57441-514-8 (ebook)
  1. Fathers and sons—United States—Poetry. 2. Fathers and daughters—United
States—Poetry. 3. Caregivers—United States—Poetry. I. Title. II. Series: Vassar
Miller prize in poetry series ; no. 20.
  PS3613.I54525C58 2013
  811'.6—dc23
                                    2012036594

Club Icarus is Number 20 in the Vassar Miller Prize in Poetry Series

for my parents, Frank and Margie
for my children, Delaney and Joseph
and for ever, Emily

"Twice he tried to engrave your fall in gold and
twice his hands, a father's hands, fell useless."

—Virgil, translation by Robert Fagles

* * *

"Mama always told me not to look into the eyes of the sun.
But, Mama, that's where the fun is."

—Bruce Springsteen

CONTENTS

AKNOWLEDGMENTS

Acknowledgment is made to the following magazines and anthologies, both online and in print, in which some of the poems in this book previously appeared (sometimes in slightly different form):

"Club Icarus" appeared in *Harvard Review, Poetry Daily*, and *New Writing of California* 2012

"Beauty of the Nail" and "Draglines" first appeared in *Literary Imagination*

"Tuggin'" first appeared in *Slate*

"Ashes" first appeared in *Cafe Review*

"The Whale" first appeared in *DMQ Review*

"Deciduous" and "Ballistics" first appeared in *Memorious: A Journal of New Verse and Fiction*

"The Devil Watches the New Idol Tryouts" first appeared in *PN Review*

"Descent of Man" first appeared in *Notre Dame Review*

"Wahine" and "Under a Bridge" first appeared in *Sea Change*

"Asante" and "Still Falling" first appeared in *The New Guard*

"A Taking Out" first appeared in *Naugatuck River Review*

"Partus" first appeared in *Mom Egg*

"Aruba, One Happy Island" and "Like Superman" first appeared in *Entelechy International*

This work was made possible by the support of Phillips Exeter Academy as well as Stanford University and the Wallace Stegner Fellowship.

Acknowledgments

I owe a debt of gratitude to many people for their critical feedback and encouragement during the writing of this book including Todd Hearon, Ralph Sneeden, Brooks Moriarty, Rusty Dolleman, Jill McDonough, Lundy Smith, Kelly Flynn, Joanna Ro, Mercy Carbonell, Joseph Hurka, Eavan Boland, W. S. Di Piero, Ken Fields, John Felstiner, Joan Houlihan, Paul Marion, Maria Hummel, Keith Ekiss, John Struloeff, Shane Book, and Alison Stine.

A very special thanks to Maggie Dietz for not only poring through every poem in this book but for giving me the faith that there was something here worth the while.

And of course for their support, for their generosity, and for their friendship, I owe everything to my family: my parents, my brothers and their families, my wife Emily and our children, Joe and Nancy Meehan, and all those who gather in Frank's Garden.

PART I

THE BEAUTY OF A NAIL

hangs on it being
unseen as when
it suspends a
painting or some
caught on camera
moment on a plain wall
or the way within
the wall it holds up
the house, the pipes,
the unrolled
insulation or even
when somewhat seen
as when it holds a man
up to martyrdom—
always it is the tool,
not the meaning.

Handwritten annotations:

become oddist.

idea: reverse painting, have a painting cut in to, attached to a wall, and hang a nail ort of it.

wall — nail — painting.

nail

behind every painting ever paid attention to the nails

nail

it does its job regardless of the job.

holds up.

beauty [of nail].

BALLISTICS

That the greasy pop-pop
of a semiautomatic wrecks

Drive-by

the air before I can get off
the couch, before my wife yanks

our baby daughter
from the new fallen flesh

of pomegranate and runs
inside before their car horrors — *Drives*

past our fence is true.
That this winter this town

has more bullets than rain
gutters in truth but is not true. But the bullets

are true. Candles, rosaries, the roses > *remembering the Dead.*
that shrine the street corner

are true beyond the next day stare
of faces watching me walk

behind a stroller. What's true
is the wound

channel, that human tissue jumps
from a bullet like water

from a diver. One
boy bled out where he fell.

The other on a table
at a university hospital. Drawn

blinds are true, checked locks. Smiles
have too much teeth to be true.

What's vital is the crush
mechanism, the permanent hole

a bullet makes in that moment
I'm watching

my wife and child each time
they fail to reach

the door. Noises at night grow
skin, grow fur, spring fangs

that scratch and score casement
glass and hinge

between what's true. And what isn't?
That I wrote down the names

of the dead, though it should be.
What's real are the costs

of moving, of staying, the recoil
from a too early doorbell,

the ten to fifteen seconds left
to a body when the heart's

instantly destroyed. What's left
is our fence five feet from

the street, the house thirty feet
from the fence, the front wall

four inches of California
bungalow and then her crib.

TUGGIN'

Whenever a nor'easter dumped
snow all night on top of town
there'd be no one in the streets
except slow groaning plows
and us, in pick ups, low-gearing
over uncleared roads and lots,
low-lifed cases of beer sliding
in the bed between our boots,
as we watched whosever turn
it was get dragged through drifts
from fifty feet of rope tied around
the trailer hitch. Chancing
speed bumps and pot holes,
you'd hold on as the truck sped
and turned, as your body rolled
and skipped along streets no longer
nameable. Legs flailed cold and
soggy. Teeth gritted a breath
above asphalt while your buddies
hooted in the back of the truck,
icy cans in their gloved hands,
lips swollen with road rash
and Skoal. The driver, always next
to go, would open it up to buck
you. He'd hard cut the wheel,
swinging you from one buried
curb to another. Or he'd just crush
down on the brakes. You'd slide
toward slack and the shine
of tail lights and fender, skidding
almost under the black rusted
axles and manifolds, rolling
away in time from a skull pop
of tires all because boys in winter
won't suffer death. Then the steel
hearted tug as the truck started up

again, as your shoulders yanked
to just short of snapping. And if
you held on your time was up
as the driver fishtailed and cast
you across the covered concrete
to bury you in a six foot bank
of snow, everyone cackling, blood
electric, all the pieces of your face
inches away from the hydrant
you wouldn't see till spring.

PALL BEARERS

We all end up the same
raw-eyed and silent six
driving back in my truck

from St. Mary's Cemetery
to a country club where
the hall has been rented.

We're tired from the standing,
the waiting, the carrying
of a weight we never knew

till then would be that heavy.
Never knew the muscle
and grip, the sweat it took,

even in a cold drizzle,
to lift it from the rollers
and hump it to the grave.

I'm not gonna make it,
someone says as we drive.
I gotta piss. We all do.

We stop at the house where
my mother is not home.
Nobody wants to go inside

the house to use the toilet,
to stand all alone staring
at the shamrock wallpaper.

Instead we shuffle out,
long coats in nice shoes,
over the black driveway,

kicking rain from the grass
in the backyard, and line up
against a wooden fence.

Finally, one of us starts.
Then one of us cracks a joke.
Then all of us are laughing

at this terrible salute as steam
rises from the puddles
we make in beds of mulch.

DESCENT OF MAN

Dear Darwin, or Charles, or Chuck, or Chaz,
I write to express my sincere derision over
the abominable state of my feet: my twisted toes,
the fused and arthritic joint on my left foot,
the stress fracture on the right, the thick and
yellow nails on both, my flattened instep arches
which pronate my ankles (so that my whole
uncle monkey body hangs its saggy weight
over nothing but a few aging, aching ligaments)
and which twist my knees and spine, tightens
my hamstrings and my Achilles tendons until
they are ready to pop. The podiatrist slobbers
at the thought of their scalpel and hammer
reconstruction. Every barefoot walk cracks
like branches as when a man falls through a tree.
I will have trouble walking at all as I get older.
Were it not for these orthotics, grown thicker
each year since I was fifteen, I would be one
of the crippled and wrecked left to huddle
alone, hungry and cold, as the rest of the tribe
follows herds across the glaciers. Instead,
I plod, breed, and eat more than I need.

DECIDUOUS

His crook of arm tenders
my head into his chest *the one who is injured.*
that slows in the morphine

bed and then I'm there, *?.*
at black of skull,
in the rhododendron

blooms where my dad
is still pulling rope
to cobble the trunk split

down the crotch by August
lightning, shattering pink
flurries onto the steam

of hemlock. On my back,
in the mulch, among my
tanks and soldiers, I squint *child.*

through flowered arms
to catch the leaking light *death ?*
of day and watch him

sweat and spit and try *which story.*
to tie off the wound.

11

FEEDING

And yet to me mornings for Frank
still begin in yellow bile and blood

breaking, burning over, eating the pink
hole in his gut where the j-tube fingerbones

out from a jejunum that's starving,
always, to be plugged into another hi-cal

sack of slurry. Eight cans a day and he can't
keep up his weight. And he stays up

all night shitting and riding a spike
of mixed-meds. Then the haunting,

the dragging of his body through
the dark halls and rooms, behind panes

of frosted glass, after the world
has collapsed into sheets. The tape

is soggy and slipping, the tube always
inching out and scratching like a thorn.

He slips into the bathroom, sits,
and at last he falls asleep then falls off

the toilet, tearing the paper skin
that wraps his knees and knuckles.

Acid, dammed behind the belly's cavity,
spills. Screams don't come but backdraft

into a suck of sighs. If he had a stomach
he would vomit. If he had a pistol he might

use it. If he could reach the pack of Lucky's
right side up on the sink he'd be okay.

Not alone. A reptile of sweat and shake,
he pushes himself to his knees, wobbles

back onto his cold, clawed feet,
moves slowly into the hall and bends

along the corridor of photos that grin
him into the gluey light of dawn.

THE WHALE

Even from the cliff
I was stung by the yellow
stink conscripting the breeze

as I descended the dunes.
A crowd had gathered
amid the darts and hooks

of blowflies to watch decay
at work in the waves.
The dead humpback, its flanks

shredded by shark or prop,
rolled sleepily in the lungcrush
of breakers slamming salt

barrels onto a beach by Half
Moon Bay. Torn fins
swung down like dock ramps

from the hill of its body. Flukes
slapped in the pounding foam,
as if a last report against death

quickly betrayed by the bladder
ballooning out of its belly
like gum blown too thin to hold.

Eyes once covenant with the sea
were shuttered to the gulls
gathering in the foggy light.

Its massive lungs burnt empty
of breath and song. Any words
we spoke died in the waves

as we looked for some measure
of life, some godswallow
of nature that still held law

in that purge of fluids,
that collapse into maggots,
that crumble of gravewax and fat.

Exempli Gratia

I want my mother to stink
of gauze, of blood, of yellow bile.

I want my forearms scabbed
and scarred from fisting death's teeth

with my brothers whose cheeks
should be hung with chunks of lung

and throat. I want us all soaking
in the seven years of breaking bowels,

wearing his scored skin, his spilling
sack of chewed food, his nest of tubes.

Something to tear our sleeves for
the questions of what happened.

STUDIES SHOW

that a mile beneath our crust these worms
not only exist but thrive in realms

of hellish heat, pressure, breathing traces
of oxygen, no sunlight, feeding
solely on bacteria and not
needing a mate to replicate.

The scientists who found them named them
Halicephalobus mephisto
because we still believe we can
bet against our Beelzebubs.

And why not when studies show
the skin of women is a window?

The deeper the wrinkle the more broken
the bones that hold up the heart
the lungs, the stomach, the bowels, the crotch

and all the hot spots where the beast
baits us with our beggar worm.

Since what are we but a pile of half baked
collagen? You can tell the journey
from the dusty jackets: a study of fossilized
teeth show women, more than men,

wandered, went, or were stolen from home
adding yet another wrinkle

on the script of our skin. Denatured down
into a faintly blushing gelatin
I slide me over the theatre lights

color my stage for Faustian friends
since studies show that glimpsing red
can make us stronger, faster, better.

At least, momentarily. It seems we humans
are hardwired to charge the passing cape,
the flushes of skin, the sudden blood.

Studies show that seeing red
improves muscular performance but
takes a mental toll on us, as
athletes facing cardinal clad
opponents tend to lose more often,
making the old myths and stories true.

Not that they never were. But back
to the science, like those worms who eat
as if they want to live on Mars.

Studies show bacteria spreading.
So what we eat is killing us.

We call for the royal taster to test
our poison but the CDC
is underfunded and can't keep up
with all the strains of pathogens
evolving around us, into us,

while below, studies show, old Mephisto
as he has done for 12,000 years,
keeps on eating what is eating us.

PART II

UNDER A BRIDGE

The tide is sucking out,
the air is hot, the harbor
crowded with boats anchored

for the afternoon. Slow adrift
in a dinghy rented too late
in the day for good fishing

are two brothers dangling worms,
a third napping in mom's
lap while dad smokes and drifts

back, gnawing the morning,
when his boys begged him to bring
them out. And when

an oar slips from his grip,
falls into the current's quick,
it is already beyond

the bow by the time he yells
"Grab it," in a voice that makes
it all her fault. And so

he stands and dives, the splash
the suck of breath before
their cries. As he is swept

under the bridge he smiles
calmly, despite his eyes.
"I can't get back," he says.

Coalish water widens.
The setting sun drips pinks
across the rivermouth.

Yelling for help, alone,
huddling her sons, mom
rows on one oar toward shore.

WAHINE

Black rubbered as a seal
she floats waist deep in winter

water. Ten or twelve men sit
with her in the lineup and weigh

the horizon for waves.
A January onshore breeze

brushes back the Atlantic lashes.
A set rises and she slides

to her belly on the longboard,
paddles into the tumor

of rolling glass, her back
arched as she digs and digs

her arms into the swelling
then drops down the face,

spray from the lip spitting
up into her eyes as she pops

liquid to her booted
feet and turns down the line,

cross-steps out to the nose,
crouches in the pocket,

fingers dipping into the curtain
to slow her speed, to pull

her deeper into the barrel
that churns, that chases,

that swaddles, that swallows,
that throats rain songs

around her. Seconds sublime but
then she peeks through the keyhole

and the witch-haired wall
of whitewater closes the door

on top of her head. The lip
explodes. She is sucked over

the falls. The muscle of the moon
crashes on her shoulders,

her back, her whole body rolled
and roiling in a soft tomb

of roaring black and brine.
Dragged down she can't break

back to the surface. Panic
tars her arteries. Arms and legs

flail. Beg to fail. Then she slows.
Stops. Lets go of fighting and

just twirls in the icy pitch
until she slips the knit

of the wave, pushes at last into air,
and swims to her board swirling

in the breakers. Her arms
noodled, her face bearded

by foam. She paddles back
into the lineup. She nods

at the men still grinning
at her fall. More water

than they are, ice
stalactites from her nose.

ARUBA, ONE HAPPY ISLAND

Too much salt for our skin but the sun
is the sun again and the sand a warm
whiteness against the stitched lip of winter
and then a woman's voice claws out
from under a beach hut like a kid drawing
on a sidewalk with a chunk of broken
mortar. It drags out of her throat
the miserable children of her miserable
children. It is as if she has shucked
their heads from off their shoulders
and piked them through on cherry
acrylics that spike from the thick
gesticulation of her hands. The heads
stare out at me from her chaise lounge.
Dopey-eyed as skeeball dolls, they beg
for someone to win them home, rescue
their smiles from her hot grave of lungs.
Her skin is brown and dry. It bat-wings
between her bones. She sips a pink drink.
My dad is two months dead and I am tired
enough for all this to be reason enough.
But her nails and hair continue to grow.
And we are here on our vacation.

PARTUS

Riflebutt the curve of her wool
socked foot into the shoulder shove

her knee down now toward her ear fingers
wrapping hamstrings stretched

now like pulled stitches
that birthmark on her knee
the flaws called the fall now

on the other side of the bed the nurse locks
hairy arms around the other leg

just a spit of chemicals
a pathology of the lonely
love now

know this if it's needed as old men
not her real doctors crouch into her
crotch now a naked spider
in the limp of fluorescents

residual feelings would be natural
aches of addiction
but hungers fade get replaced

walk out right now
into a dead stomach winter
at this hour of the morning no one cares
for what disappears forever

the baby now by heaving rips out
brown and beet now
so much more rip and twist
from thighs lights her hot swell of earth

focus on the scissors the slick purple
and grey of the cord
now so much black

blood should there be so much
black blood and no crying

starched hush then little hacks
at air the chokes on spots of oxygen
how long now since the water

broke how many times do you need
to say now in a hospital
not now stop now please now

not breathing right he says *emergency now*
what is it she says

leave now before anything
can be lost in the scraping

at air *yes it's a girl*
is she all right now which she

the doctor digs rubber gloves back into her

more bleeding down here than I like
to see scissors thread now
old hands snip now winces rip

her face now *see if she's okay make her*
be okay she says now

run down a hall as if hip deep in mud
walls implode NICU doors blow

open into a pool of blue swimmers
too small for March now don't feel
bad feeling good she is not one

of them *now this way daddy*
someone says and now her eyes
open staring wet and we are

breathing right here terrified beautiful
now for what the world will take

OLD LAD IN THE CASTLE

Just wait. My nuclear samurai second,
my chance to pump out the radioactive
water, to keep the fuel rods cool
and save the little glowing bottles
of baby milk, approaches. I don't know
what millisieverts are but I'll happily burn
my skin in them. Just give me the chance.
Yes, that's what I need. A moment
of catastrophe. Then I'll be my hero
and all of this circuit and light
will have been earned. Then no more
the thunder-stone, the winter's rages,
the torn Achilles, tau, and old age homes.
Where is my collection of earthquakes,
my bombed out schools, my blight?
There must be a market for disaster
tourism—a place for us to also feel
all that heat, to throat that tyrant's rope
we've watched grow between glows of dust.
Hit me as hard as I can charge on my card.
Give me something to force my petal
to the mettle, to satisfy this soft
wondering of fists against the posts.
This is what I'll ask of my Wizard,
my Secret Santa, my Great Pumpkin,
my General Patton, my Charlie Chaplin.
Although I'm sure I will, while staring
at some screen or line, miss the chance
when it shows up. Or at least that's how
I'll reconcile the pale quiver in my liver,
the fall of my staff followed by a quipped
cover up as I keep up the long look out
for my Godzilla to tsunami from the sun.

CANDY LAND

Let's say your mom buys you a gift,
say it's a board game, say it's Candy Land,
and you're still a kid, a boy, barely four,
it's Florida and it's hot out but it's not
your birthday, just a kindness by her.
And suppose you refuse it, the gift,
the game she slides out of a store bag.
You yell and spit and throw it in her face
which is for the first time destroyed
by something you can do and say you've
been feeling small, say you already know
you're a weakling in a world of crowding
and you're afraid already of your skinny
wrists and Candy Land seems girly to you,
too pink and rainbow although gum drop
islands and molasses tar pits do sound
delicious. But say you lie to be tough
and crush out your mother's smile and
she puts the gift back in the bag and returns
it or gives it to the mom of a neighbor's
kid. And so you never play Candy Land.
And say you don't play your whole life.
Say you do these things to her your whole
life. Say you see yourself starting
to do things like this to your wife, acting
as if a man is made from yell and spit.
Say you see your daughter smile and think
what if someday she asks you to play
Candy Land. What will you say? Will you
be that boy again? Will you arrive at what
it is, a man? Will you sit on the floor
with her and play and not yell and spit
because it's too late for the boy, not
too late to just say thank you and play.

A Taking Out

With stiff knuckled fists she pulls
then twists the trash bag ends,
yanks them up into a knot, wincing

in its eggy gasp, and shucks
the bag from the waste basket to lug
it through the kitchen door. She tumbles

the stink down on top of the others,
into one of the barrels that will blow
all around the street before anyone

bothers to bring it back down a driveway
scabbed with ice. Breakfast is done.
The boys are off to school and her father

is dead. Her father is dead and above
her the elm branches are dried spiders
against this sun. She feels gravel

in her slippers, her throat. She turns back
up the driveway and coughs into a whip
of wind and does not weep

for her father dead, for elbows
that ache every evening, for her husband's
boring baldness, for her boys needing

her less, for all this in a thin blue
robe she pulls tight around the soft middle
that has become her mother, the lumps

of her that his fingers steal over only
in a malted dark, that arms no longer
tug and tug at. But it's a fine winter

morning. Bright, crisp, like a smiling stranger
whose approach up her walk she
does not recognize but suddenly expects.

DRAGLINES

I'm up before the baby.
   Outside it's still

      dark, still raining.
   Ankles pop and click

to the bathroom where
   I sway and piss

still seeing
   last night's news:

      A mother drowned
   her three sons:

Stripped them then dropped
   them into the San Francisco Bay.

      Moving to the shower
   I twist the knobs. On the wall

a spider spilling silk
   smacks against the tiles

      from the crush of water.
   Witnesses said they didn't see

her roll away
   an empty stroller.

She clings to mildew
   as her broken filigree

   is slurped into the earth
      underneath my feet.

She'd been hearing the voices
   of angels all day.

      In the hiss of steam
does she watch

   through eight eyes

from eight angles

her sac of eggs torn away,
     sucked down?

          Did she hear
          a last gulp of apology

from the one old enough
     to believe

that there must
     be a reason?

In a flood of storm
     and whirlwind,

as the world gets ready
     to leave for work,

     as I scrub the film
          from my skin

     as my daughter
begins to wake and cry,

the spider holds
     a dry corner to her belly.

THE DEVIL WATCHES
THE NEW IDOL TRYOUTS

The daylong auditions were held
in one of the last abandoned
shipyard warehouses during the mean
middle of winter and were judged
by a panel of eight, mostly men—
Ivy MBA-looking types in dark suits
and leather sandals. Arriving together
on one bus, some of the older gods
were there to try out, bringing
with them their quivers of lightning,
goatskin drums and pipes, masks
and feathers, lamps, mistletoe, flaming
swords and all kinds of crosses. Sadly,
some of them had gotten hair plugs
or wore girdles to hold back great
golden bellies and the amazed look
on their faces betrayed a conspiracy
of Botox injections. They all got equal
time. Most of them nailed
their lines but none of them earned
even the hope of a call back.
They never really had a shot. Every part
to be cast called for someone, well,
younger, sleeker, with more soft
lights and switches, gods you plugged
into your skin, that came with GPS
and their own soundtracks, gods
that you could stick in a vein or swallow
like a baby stone, that were user friendly,
that had bundled add-ons and cheap
accessories for quick customization.
All pimped out in plastic and chrome
and chanting static, the young gods
were cocksure as they read for roles
from chemical to coaxial. Most

hadn't even bothered to look over
the script. It didn't matter,
because they sure looked good.
And they had tested well
with consumers ages six to sixty-six.
With orders to fill, the judges couldn't
help but show them their teeth.

CONSIDER

Consider the category of the lunged
metaphor, enough breath left to lie.
Yes, man and mockingbird, parrot of air,
the chameleon's cafeteria is open.

Consider that we are taught to trust
our eyes, that your hands are
the last part to say goodbye, and why
we eat love out of trashcans.

Consider that each particle is distraction
from God, that there is no God and this detail
of the "I" is a scratched lens, that
the eye believes too much of its truth.

Remember it is all collapsing when you
discuss color, when taste gets no simile,
that the object is closer to the verb
than it appears in the compact of syntax.

Accept that you are the machine of death,
the last finger on the trigger, the hand
chalked with all of our wiped names,
the one out back stacking a cord of limbs.

CLUB ICARUS

We're no more than a few silver
seconds in the air when that winged
and cocky boy gets sucked   b. rd.
into a turbine sparking off a fire
that rips the starboard wing
away from the fuselage, shucking
passengers out and raining
us over Northern California, dozens
of us dropping towards the bay
and you can imagine the screams,
I'm sure, the prayers cast up
then down the twirling sky,
and yet here's my daughter
laughing the whole way
down, her yellow hair whipping
around her first teeth smile,
as she titters at the tilted
wonder of what was happening,
rolling airborne over and over,
as we all drop like sacks of wet
clay and for a second I want to snag
her, to show her how frightened
she should be, so I can hug
her safe one last time, but the way
she looks laughing I just can't
and so as the brick of the bay
comes up to kiss my back I watch
my little girl giggling, grinning
floppy-cheeked into the wind
and then, damn, if I don't see, right
before the world splits my sides,
wings like blades butterfly
from her back and lift her
laughing back into the blue.

set up like
a straight fall.

PART III

A DEMOCRACY OF DEVILS

The Asian Tiger is weak
as flyers go, a lifetime
radius of maybe two
hundred yards and yet
made in Taiwan, made
in Vietnam, she is now
in Lebanon, and here
she is in Italy, in France
in Bolivia, Spain, Cuba,
and the Netherlands
and in '85 coming
to Houston in a crate
of recapped tires, lands
now in old New Bedford
where Novembered Ishmael
sailed toward Nantucket.
A spring of dumping rain
wakes her season early.
Aggressive as a fever
she is the forest day
mosquito, not hiding
in the woods until
ballpark dusk to suck,
nor slipping the hide flaps
of our morning tents.
She prefers the human
city: the plugged roof

gutters, old tires holding
water, roadside trash,
those bird baths forgotten,
sewers and flower pots:
all the wrappers of our
sugar. Only the female
needs the blood meal
but she cannot drink
full for her eggs in one
feeding so she jumps
hosts, becomes a vector
for West Nile virus,
for dengue fever and
encephalitis. The jungle
of pathogens paved to stay
away come silver striped,
flits into our baby yards,
organized around a diet
of invention and need.
Does she share our mad?
Need she harpoon a god?
Can this small brain think
thoughts? Desire a coupled
hell? Drag the judge at last
to the bar? At least then
there would be justice
in ovitraps and DEET.
Would the old algebra
add up: eye for eye,
a leg for an egg. For we
are eating up all the nests.
North and west shrinks
even as it expands.
Ah, were this the reason,
the cause, for what's in karma's
velvet paws. But there's shit
beyond what is written
on these dusty cells;
this the only handspike

that digs into the masts,
that winches the windlass.
No, we are not the whale
nor meant to be a part
of good and evil's big
budget productions. There
are no villains, just the quick
and then the extinction.
For the redundant mobs,
the brains begin to swell
with febricity or the fog.
The bat houses are filled
with white flags and while
there is hope some say
in the Anisoptera
only our coughing children
still believe in dragons.

TRIGGERS

[handwritten: for what?. drugs.]

Across patches of pitch and grease
softening on August's hot
top parking lot I trip a path
past Bobcats, blowers, and Scags,

skirting the teeth of rusted out
thatchers and push at last
past frosted glass into Lowell
Rental. I've come for a drop *[handwritten: refrences drugs?]*

spreader to throw some Dylox on
the grubs still chewing up
my lawn. Behind the register
a fat woman flicks her tongue

along the edges of an ice
cream cone. Vanilla streaks
down a cookie dough roll of wrist.
A tank top drapes toward red

denim thighs. I finally catch her eyes.
"Hey, please don't tell my boss,"
she says through a hack of phlegm and cream
"I'm really not supposed

[handwritten: Control] to eat at work but I am so
hungry." I nod and tell
her why I'm here. She slides a form
across Formica and calls

for Lenny on the intercom.
I grab a pen from a mug.
"I hate myself," she says to me,
though I'm not looking up.

"I used to be a bodybuilder."
I do look up. And she
[handwritten: Opening] points out a Polaroid of a ripped
and tanned version of her

pinned behind her on the wall
of cork crowded by dirty comics
and pizza coupons. I gaze up at
a glaze of muscles, the bleached   *artificial?*

white teeth, the peroxide hair teased up
to frame the same green eyes
looking at me now. "I used to
work out everyday. Then

I started shooting up." I don't
know what to say to her
or why she's telling me all this
or if she's shitting me.   *might be lying.*

Vanilla drips onto her lap.
"I really hate to eat
from cones but I can't use a cup
because I'd need a spoon.

The spoon's a trigger. I can't have spoons
around or I'll want to cook
up. Can't even have spoons at home.
My kids all have to eat   *~~food~~ need to work.*

Froot Loops with forks." "That sucks," I say
imagining the ache
of watching milk silk through the prongs   *slip what does it evoke?*
"Everyday at school my kids

get teased because of their fat mom.
But it's okay since I'm
going to get my stomach stapled.
As long as I don't lose   *herself sobriety.*

this job." I finish filling out
the form. "So, please don't tell
no one I was eating, okay?"
I slip her fifty bucks—

the deposit—and pocket the pen. Lenny
rolls out my rental. "I won't   *?*
tell anyone," I say and leave
with my spreader of poison.

43

BLIND MAN

He hangs in the library window
like some storefront crucifixion,

his left arm extended out to hold
the miniblind track in place while

the right, reaching the other way,
pushes a drill against the frame joint

to shriek a screw through aluminum
and into the brick wall behind.

Shoved together on the last step
of the step ladder, steel toes balance

in a scrambling sun. Sweat beetles
down his face, fogging his glasses,

darkening his red shirt at the chest,
across his back, and in all the pits

of his body. Freckled arms burn
and shake, pale wet hairs soaking

up dust as he leans over the glass.
The wail of burrowing metal rises,

cuts past his ears and into the stacks.
Sighs rise from laptops and lamps,

from their copies of Whitman, Zinn.
He's asked to be quiet or come back

at a *more appropriate hour*. He nods
but continues to drill, until the last

screw squeaks to a stop, the threads
snagging in the anchor ribs. Exhaling,

he wipes an itch from his forehead
and climbs down the ladder, grunting

and stretching knots from his back.
"All set," he says to anyone listening.

Then he grabs the cord and gives it a light
tug, snuffing out the morning glares

with the tinny gasp of falling slats.

PARADOXICAL UNDRESSING

Who you are stands in the snow
with no name and no face and a voice
only the ice can echo.

I am you that loved the world once
in spring with mud between fingers
and toes. I was naked then and knew

it but did not care. They say the falling
of the leaves taught me shame
but that is not how I remember my skin,

slippery in the dry autumn paper.
My lungs were cool; I could run
forever if I wanted to.

But you are not me. I am no fool
to perch there in a field of blizzard
and watch the cold glow

from the brick-eyed windows.
There is no air in here but we sleep
fine in our blue and orange lights.

CORRECTIONS

So this kiddy diddler sharpens a spoon, strips,
and starts candy caning

his arms and legs as he hums, twitches
and grins in the back

of his cell waiting for me to tug myself
into this bite suit that's supposed

to protect me from the blade and poison
blood leaking from his skinny,

greasy, white as a wedding cake
body. Two other guards, both without

wives and with even fewer hours
in than me pad up too since, lucky us,

we get to go in and save this ass ripping
rapist from killing himself quicker

by beating the ever living loving hell
out of him. And so we pounded

away until he stopped squirming,
stopped smiling, until my hands stopped

hurting and I started running
out of places to hit

and there was nothing left of that sick
prick but a purple bubbling.

Until he was subdued. Saved. They washed
blood and skin off our suits. Stripped,

I went back to my post on D. My knuckles
sore as shit. My hands shaking.

I couldn't get them to stop
shaking. For hours. Even after I snuck

a snort in the can, they kept twitching,
like they weren't ever mine.

LIKE SUPERMAN

From slick covered stacks
of capes and masks a boy begins
the walk to school with ganglions
blitzing comic book kinetics.
One step bat, next step spider, fists
popping claws, carrying shields
and totem boomerangs, he walks
the rooftop ledge of sidewalks swinging
across greenlight crosswalks on webs,
on hooks, on wings, on fire, and hunts
the menaces of world and city to save
the girl in second period math who sits
next to him and smells like berries.
Then somewhere the pulp yellows
into grey. Those bright colors
of his bad guys dull to everyday.
And he figures out evil
is historical, subtle, and not
to be found in the hysterical
smile of clowns drawn in gloss
brigades of paint and ink.
No monsters. No madmen on the fringe.
No easy enemy to swoop down upon.
Just debt, taxes, and acid reflux while
charcoal men wage cartoon wars.
Still, he thinks it would be nice
if he could feel his thumbs press
into the throat of a purple villain
to win a kiss from that girl
in math who smells like berries.

SEE YOU IN THE FUNNY PAGES

newspaper narrator.

Fold me up at last into this globe
of blue ideas and tilted axes, *the mind?*
seal the top back on and set
me spinning across the pitch,

that scaffold of dark matter physicists *evil stuff*
have finally found, but which is all
around and has always been right
here showing up most recently orange-   *crazy guy killed people.*

haired at a movie theater in Colorado
to say *Riddle me this, Batman*
with 6000 rounds at 50 rounds a minute. *— guns*
What's happening to our baby boys? *— culture of violence*

Why keep pulling them into lockers
and hurt showers? Who lets this happen?
Lacerations on the palms are defense *— cutting?*
wounds, not the marks of Jesus.

Why aren't our girls and sad eyed
Sal Mineos throwing flowers   *maybe the outward achievement*
at the husks inside the red jackets? *but emotional void?*
I've lost you, I know, I'm sorry. *why? what have you done?*

look toward the boys, not weapons.   I'm looking for the language *— what do they mean.*
of bullets but the bullets themselves
are more accessible, a lot cheaper,
and so much the quicker way

to make a difference in the lives   *strong embodiment of America*
of others. What can Captain America
do against stiff onshore winds? *inavailable*
One painted shield is no good

against a thousand gunmen shouting
fire inside a theater, inside a school, *new town*
suicide? inside their own heads over and over,
each voice another minute under water.
— we need to listen

48

The Best Defense

Dragonflies cut black and red
across the blue-tipped afternoon
above a mown to gold October

grass that's being trampled under
the cleats of big grunting boys.
The old line coach climbs the back

of the six-man blocking sled.
His eyes are hidden by silver
sunglasses, his face shadowed

by a hat, his arms wrapped
in long grey sleeves. He needs
to keep the sun from his skin,

to keep in his gut his morning blast
of chemo sick. The boys crouch,
four-point stances, one boy per

each bag slung over iron slabs
curving up from the ground.
At the coach's sudden whistle

they lunge like starving dogs.
Feet drive and dig into dirt.
Thick, scabbed hands punch

up into the bags. Two tons
of red iron reels up and back.
The coach leans into it and

blasts the whistle. The boys
drop to the ground, backwards
onto their asses, and spin left,

rolling back up into stances
in front of another bag and fire
out again as the next blow

shrills the air. Blood, sudden
but not unexpected, trickles,
unnoticed by the players,

leaves the coach's right nostril.
Another whistle blast hides
a curse. He stuffs his nose

with tissue. He tries to shoo
away two dragonflies threading
around him. His lungs feel thick

yet thinning. His head fills with nails.
Again the whistle. Coupling
into one, the dragonflies drag

at each other to hang on his shirt.
A long tweet ends the drill. Huffing,
spitting, the boys stand, hands

on hips, mouth pieces hanging
from facemasks. "Hey, coach,"
says the starting center, "Two

dragonflies are screwing on
your shoulder." The coach climbs
off the sled and looks across

the field, toward the rusty line
of trees. "It happens," he says
and lets his boys take a knee.

TRUE STORY

The last time I got with God
I was stinkass drunk.

So was he. And when
we finally left the clubs

and got back to my place
it got a little rough.

I mean he was always
into dirty talk and silk knots

but this was a little more
than just make-up sex.

It was a full on hate-fuck.
Which, okay, I get.

And I got it, head to toe,
scratched and bruised.

But what skeeved me
out the most

was when, while riding
me, he pulled my cock

out from his pussy
and stuck it up

his own asshole,
This was a first for me.

The next morning—God
is the stay the night

and cuddle kind—
he laughed and told me

"You really tore up my insides."
That pretty much sealed

it up for me and the whole
personal Jesus idea.

ASANTE

Asante, you dropped the ball.
Asante, you son of a bitch.
An interception would have ended
the drive, saved us from the helmet catch,
the loss, the upset.
Asante, I keep seeing it in my dreams.
Asante, I needed that win.
Asante, my brothers needed it. My mother.
Asante, my father in his lucky shirt watched every game
that season, died the day after
you won the divisional playoffs against Jacksonville.
Asante, we watched him dying as we watched the game
we were supposed to go to on the hospital television.
Asante, when the paramedics came to his house
they tore open his lucky shirt and when he was revived
he was pissed off you should have seen how skinny
his anger had become eating through that tube
threaded into his gut that burned his skin in bile.
Asante, we watched him breathe to death.
Asante, you held out for more money.
Did that dropped ball have something to do
with the missed practices? Did you get paid enough?
Asante, the NFL is America.
Asante, the NFL is a beautiful high-class hooker.
She takes all my money but shows me a good time.
Asante, ticket prices went up again.
Asante, I paid for you to drop the ball.
Asante, my father got season tickets in 1981 when nobody
wanted to go and pissed-off fans threw grills on the field.
Asante, I am the NFL. I fucked myself with my fantasy team.
Asante, my father taught me fatherhood teaching me to catch
a football bulleted between the trees in the Ashby woods.
I bounced off the trees. Asante, "It hurts more when you
    drop it, eh?"
said a smile and a cigarette and a bright sun through the pines.
Asante, he could throw a ball so hard you should have seen it.
Asante, he was left handed except when he wrote.

Asante, I joked it was a good thing he died because that game
would have killed him. Asante, did you know that Eli
is the Hebrew word for God? Asante, Asante, lama sabachthani?
Asante, I could not sleep for months without seeing
replay replay replay of the ball bouncing off your hands.
Asante, there should have been something I could have done.
Should I have made them stop? Hook the ventilator back up?
Would he have gotten better? Asante, he was not getting better.
Asante, he told a friend but not his sons he was sick of fighting.
Asante, I went to my first game when I was eight. My dad
took us and my brother got yelled at by someone behind us
for getting up too often to go get food.
Asante, we were all thin then but my father.
Asante, you are just a number. Asante, my father was a
        handsome man.
Asante, I figured out the dream had nothing to do with you.
Asante, I figured it out minutes before I watched my wife's
grandmother—102!—breathe herself to death her lips pulled back
like my dad's did you know I was the last
one to leave the hospital room? As I left two kids
tried to come in, they had the wrong room, my dad
would have laughed his unthreading lungs off
to have seen them scared shitless by his withered corpse.
Asante, I think my mom needed it to be over
but she would never say so.
Asante, this is poetry you will never read it.
Asante, I am profiling. I played football too.
Asante, did you know your name comes from the Ashanti
of western Africa? Do you know about the Golden Stool?
Is your soul safe? Asante, my father couldn't sit on a toilet
without shitting razorblades. Asante, do you trace your lineage
through your mother? My mother's father played
for the Green Bay Packers. Asante, I am a poet.
Asante, I am through with your nightmare.
Asante, my son is crying I have to go.

PART IV

A Murmur of Birds

In the hot belly of a summer morning
the assembly hall filled. All the audience
was children. Nothing was air-conditioned.
Brochures for colleges were used as fans and sweat
swam in mingling pools between thighs and necks.

After an hour or so of waiting, of laughter turning
to yawning, turning to grunting "shits" and passing
outs in aisles, the speaker began to speak
of apocalyptics and of service to man. The Power
Point slid between severed baby heads,

chicken wired clits, and other noble causes.
The speaker was both a handsome Caucasian male
and a fiery Asian woman who knew
how to sell it. The Asian yelled and the white
guy cried apologies. The children napped.

They knew this all already. The had taken
some of the photos themselves. They could
spot their fathers' handiwork anywhere.
They knew it all and knew by now they would
forget it all in any moment that might matter.

Their wisdom was as headstone as their hearts.
Some began to look out at the flaking black
charcoal sky and wonder what the dining hall
was serving for lunch. A couple of the kids started
fucking. They wanted to get all this over with.

MORTICIAN'S BALL

Your ice wagon diesels through fusillade
racing rigor mortis, racing the Persian sun
as you enter an orchestra of flak and thunder,

of bones bowing string and fiber, of a chorus
caught in chemical sear, of hymns hacked
and gasped, of drums split open like bellies

of oil burning day into night, of the lightning
trumpets of 155s, of milky eyes tinkling
the shrapnel, of the ball, the battle and you

spill out into the fire with a bag and trowel
to tango your angels, these dead marines,
from the rip of metal. Uranium rounds sing

into cells as you crawl under a Hummer
blown and burning. Already the cheese,
the crust of lips, the black pools growing

as you pick a partner out of the dirt,
hold together what's left. Drag him, drag
her, back to the truck, back to the hangar

of slabs, to knit and stitch some soul back
onto this crush of flesh. Some are friends,
all are brothers, all have mothers who don't

want to cry over closed caskets. *Look, your kid
didn't suffer for a second.* Sew up those last
seconds. *And anyway, marines don't die,*

regroup in hell. Taking care of my brothers
you tell your family back home in Lawrence
where maybe your wife teaches ballroom

in the same hall you host wakes for the family
funeral parlor. Nothing new about death
but *No one dies peacefully in their sleep*

over here. Over here, send the Yanks, send the
sagging pouches of flesh and effects puzzled
out in the streets. A sonogram slips

from the pocket of a dead kid who'll never
see his own kid and images of your kids
pirouette in the dust and guts of your nights.

But all the king's horses and all the king's men,
you hear your little girl singing as you tuck
her in. A bed of color-coded flags stabbing

the earth to keep track of the piles, keep track
of your friends, your family, *Couldn't put
Humpty together again.* One-eighty-four,

the number of dead counted on your hands,
and then you're shipped back to the turn
and whirl of family, of work, of God

and country, of headaches and shakes,
of dawnwatch nights, of pills that don't help,
of the farandole of faces, the shots you fire

into the nightclub street. *Foxtrot. Tango.*
One-eighty-four. How much a year takes.
How long the ball lasts. And then the music

breaks up. Dancers part, depart, go home
in gowns. But there was never any music.
And never any dancing in the infrared dirt.

12 OZ. KOOZIE

cut off the nose to spite the face
= krella.

Say God and spite the face.
Which story will replace you today?

an idea, mask?

You are darkness.

What is beyond the whiteness and what listens
after that? Every morning the crunch

inevitability of nature.

of workers clearing away the ice storms.
The winds are bigger than ever before

natures Progression

and water works to take back its spine
of land. Indian giver. The river is not

we are doing it ourselves

rising. We are sinking. So swallows
the throat. This tenement of rock and loam

Our time is at an end...

is in foreclosure. Sharks and roaches
are at the auction but can't outbid the frog

waiting.

killing fungi. So watch your inhales
in the low tide sand, eternal as iron

drowning.

or paper, as the sea turns us past blue,
then swirls and turtles our leaky cradle.

turns it upside down

not responsible, in our
infancy

ICARIAN

After the first ever backside
720 across a seventy-foot-gap

Jake Brown in a slide
loses his board at the ramp's

vertical lip and rises
50 feet up into the air

hangs there
for maybe a single frame

of film then falls
arms and legs flapping

in the angel instinct
still written on our cells

and he watches as the wood
races to toward his face

until he turns to let the meat
of his body hit

the ramp bottom ribs
broken lung punctured

wrist fractured
his shoes blown off

he laid there as dead still
as the thrilled and

silent crowd
then he got up and walked

I guess there was some luck
involved

he told the TV later I'm happy
to be talking to you

and I'm psyched I nailed
that 720

WATER HAZARD

You know about the plastic island,
not the mind nor some insular Tahiti,
but the one we made off the coast
of California? So now there's a ban
on dumping plastic into the Pacific
and now the people are no longer
allowed to hit golf balls from the decks
of cruise ships. This is a severe blow
to the economy of vacations, enough
so that there is funding for research.
Now fear no more, a recent article reads,
a university has invented a new ball
made from lobster shells. It will sink
and dissolve within weeks and all
will be well for the human experiment.
While the lobster laments already the trap
he may wonder at this quintessence
of claw when after the bucket, the boil,
the butter and the waste basket he is
rolled into a ball and hit back into his cradle
of sea. He may pause and wonder who
left the lights on and us in charge. But no,
he is a lobster and likely doesn't even own
his own scream. And really we are all
pulled out of the abyss just to be hit
back in off the deck of some cruise ship
and in between the trap and the deck
we build islands out of leftover ideas.

BIRDING

I do not know the old songs
sung for the morning by the morning

birds in the little patch of trees
beyond our bedroom window.

I do not know birds
and have never known birds

or what they sing and which
sings what. I've seen the robin

and the cardinal in the day
but do they throat the dawn

with whistles, chortles, rattles
and croaks? I do not know

if I would know the difference
between such curling sounds.

I have seen a heron stare through
time atop a river stone

while gulls darted fish in the dirty
waters below the old leather

mill as midday cooked. But what,
or if, they sing I've never heard.

I had a friend who taught me
the turkey vulture circling

but not its noise. The great blue
heron's flight is silent

just above the Squamscot
behind the glass framed photo.

In the rough and shadowed pines
is that a Blue Jay's rusty pump?

Does a purple martin croak
courtship before the light

comes through the sugar
maples? I do not know.

I have never learned and
wonder would it matter if I had

known the gurgles, the gutturals,
or the chipping of sparrows.

I cannot say if the red-tailed hawk
from his perch on the dying oak

hisses for his lust or for the hunt
of house mice.

I have heard the mourning dove
but did not know that it was.

I can play poorly with their words,
play the mockingbird, but

I only know that the dusky crows
caw and caw the twilight as dogs

bray on chains and the Downeaster
blows its horn north for Durham.

And I've heard the crush of quiet
following the splash when feathers fail.

Kettle of Fish

I

I am something of an onion cutter,
one of those boys made to row lifeboats away

from unsinkable ships. Of wide-brimmed
hats and pins we've had enough and gin

to spare but don't come at it like that.
The lessons are boring in real time.

Edit to fit your attention, measure once
and cut, cut, cut. I am folding into my own

biography. I am part of the floor, part of the chair
where I learned to tie knots around my feet.

II

You're still here, very well, the attic is
warmer this time of year. Watch the blizzard

barrels roll into the shore. Oh, to be that cave
of sharks and sea lions. I would a tongue

to taste every man and woman I salt.
And who hung these portraits? Who ever

hangs portraits? Does anyone stand
anymore for such manipulations of light,

such erasure of time and are they hiring
hands with hooks down at the docks?

III

Was anyone left in the house when you woke?
Was that what made you mad or happy,

or was there something else? I feel blue
is an easy color to explain but try yellow

and you rivet a valley where the sun
crowns out of the earth and burns through

the crotches we spent all night gently rubbing,
divining, with bent wires. And quite a sun it is

we have brought upon ourselves to capture tears,
whiplash the sea, and boil the baby in its fluid.

MIDDLE FLIGHT

From a distance, from the little black
shades he wears, his brown eyes
look shot out, like eyes of a tanned skull.

But get closer and he is just James Bond.
The photo is 3 X 6. It is far too small
for a wall, too wobbly for a desk.

Belonging nowhere it ends up
everywhere and I find them again
one morning ten years later,

unpacking boxes from another move,
these four men, smiling out
against a backdrop of fence and ivy.

The frame is cheap, tinted gold,
and loose around the little photo of us
on a back deck in black tuxes

a few hours before a graduation gala
at Union Station for Paul who takes
the center weight of the shot. His right

hand wraps around a can of Bud
as he curls a smile. More of the white
of his shirt shows than on the rest

of us. And he is straighter than us,
who have done this already somewhere else.
It is his grinning eyes that first lock

into you. Jon slumps coolly in a lawn
chair, lower than all of us, in the left hand
corner. Almost all black, almost all

shadow in his closed coat and arms.
His eyes are shut as tight, his lips
as full, as a corpse or a drunk.

Yet not dead, and not yet drunk, he is
just caught in a blink by the photographer.
He curls a smile, his legs are crossed

like my father's though, unlike my father's,
right over left. In the far right, leaning in,
leaning on my leaning father in imperfect

parallel, I do my best dash of smile,
my left hand holding my right wrist,
my straight hair in a stiff curl of gel.

In the photo I am taller than my father,
but leaner. He is big, his tanned face
is wide and grinning my grin.

In a week he will collapse on a green,
his stomach exploding into his guts.
And he will never be hungry

again and he will always be too
thin and the thin will kill him. But here,
in this shot, one week before his seven

years yellow in hospitals and bile,
he is large. Larger than us. And in his hands
that curl a heart, he nurses a beer.

IN THE BONES

Up on the hill the bubble gum
of her pink winter coat is mashed
against the concrete sky. She kneels
in the moss of the old cemetery.
My daughter has never run away
before but I remember how

to run away looks like. And so
I squish through our mire of yard,
step past the breaking lilac

of crocus pushing up despite
the late March slush and snow.
I climb the hill, up the underbrush,

to where her head hangs down
in front of the stone of Abigail Thing,
"Died 1765." A winged death head

crowns the marble slab and pulling
at a stripped finger of pine root
my daughter says she wants to see

a skeleton: "Not the fake ones
at the museum." I scare her
when I say to dig Abigail up

means her ghost will come to haunt.
I want her to know the mystical
which means to fear the mystical

but the nightmares are already
at the edges of her eyes so I say
that will not happen, the ghost

will not happen. But I scare her
by saying the police will come
if we dig up the bones of Abigail.

"They'll arrest us and we won't see
Mommy anymore?" she says and I
have to tell her that this will not

happen, the police will not happen.
But she is looking for the ghosts 2
and she is looking for the police 3

and she had run away today
because I yelled at something
she did but I do not remember

what it was but it was enough — *something in the fist.*
to scare her up this hill to root
true bones among the dead.

STILL FALLING

The dark is the burlap
bagging your head
in hot breath hard
to breathe with that rope
around your throat
and then the floor quits
and you gasp for the slack
to cut out but there's nothing
but the dark and a breeze
between your knees
and you're still falling
through all your seams
those things you didn't do
with that girl who smiled
from the other escalator
the son you wouldn't have
the book you couldn't write
the tree you didn't climb
in Levine's yard even
if your little brother did
but you're still falling
wintering really down
and down and bored
with it all you decide
to learn French the fiddle
when to nine iron
and when to wedge
how it feels to be faithful
to your wife how it feels
to not be how much sugar
Kool Aid needs when to tear
down the tree house
they never used and that
the universe is flat
and still falling no stopping
no sudden crackle spit

and wiggle so you drop
into thought for a thousand
years give or take a yo yo's
length of string realizing
it's easy to be a holy man
at the working end of a noose
while your hood slips
off into a lilac evening
and you work out the math
for why the universe is
flat why umpires believe
the bat, why that smile
became your wife why
your kids still think to call
why Kool Aid is the greatest
compliment you can give
to sugar and why the breeze
between your knees is warm
without the devil and when
you do come down to this
when you do see the summer
finally curling pink
upon the waves
you'll know the rest
will be a snap

ASHES

Tell me the pocketknife
left over from a dream.

Tell me about black bread,
pork and beans, stains

of cigarettes on your heavy
mesh jersey. Tell me

winter was anomaly,
tell me moss and willow.

Hip deep in the brook,
stones are eggs you tell me

this and then we lean
into the dragon of play.

Shadows tell me
where catfish crawl. Jump

you tell me by the mud
where the wasp star digs.

Tell me how to whittle
sticks into what shapes

I will. Tell me there are coals
left for your lungs.

The falls are too close,
tell me louder the grass

has not grown over
your brown earth of eyes.

Tell me out of the tunnels.
Tell me the sun,

the wax. Tell me again
about the water.

CPSIA information can be obtained at www.ICGtesting.com
Printed in the USA
LVOW06s1447110713

342468LV00008B/1044/P